A governing board can scarcely function well without an occasional opportunity to step back from its routine business agendas for an in-depth look at the institution's future. Too often, the assumption that trustees are reluctant to set aside additional time becomes an excuse for not conducting a retreat—a self-fulfilling prophecy. Board members will respond to reasonable requests for their time and attention if they believe their time will be used well.

Richard T. Ingram, *Trustee Orientation and Development Programs*

Governing boards seldom have time to pause during their routine work for an in-depth examination of the organization, its environment, its future, or for a searching look at board effectiveness. A retreat offers an opportunity for refocusing on fundamentals, thoughtful long-term planning, and reflection on mission, vision, and strategic goals. Retreats strengthen trust and relationships among board members and between the board and staff. A retreat can pull together a divided board on an issue crucial to the future of the organization. Carefully planned retreats, usually held at least once a year, are a critical component in the ongoing process of building an effective board. The knowledge, spirit, and common sense of direction that often emerge from a retreat benefit the board long after the sessions end.

Boards that regularly engage in retreats know their value, but boards that either do not hold retreats or have suffered bad experiences may question the expenditure of time and money. A board retreat should be viewed as an investment in excellence. A typical board volunteers thousands of hours a year, while executive staff spend numerous hours preparing for board activities. A

1

periodic retreat is a small additional investment that can pay tangible dividends, such as a more informed board, clearer organizational direction, better board-executive relationships, and more efficient board meetings.

Retreats offer an occasion for planning and team-building that simply cannot get done amidst the assembly line of budgets, policies, updates, and oversight of the typical board agenda. To persuade skeptical trustees or the executive of the value of investing in a retreat, seek the advice of other boards that have had successful retreats. Ask about their retreat-planning process and the positive outcomes. Seek advice from nonprofit associations and governance consultants with experience in board retreats. Finally, consult other books and articles written about board retreats (see Suggested Resources).

Ingredients of Success

A successful board retreat is a product of commitment, objective-setting, planning and preparation, data-gathering, and finally, the conduct and follow-up of the retreat. This booklet traces the retreat process from start to finish. (See Appendix A for a visual representation of this process.) A summary checklist and sample retreat planning tools will help executives and board members organize a productive retreat (see Appendix B for a checklist).

STEP 1: SECURE COMMITMENT

As with any other endeavor, top-level commitment is essential to the success of a board retreat. Commitment is based on the belief that a retreat will enhance the effectiveness of the board and the organization. The board takes its cue from how the chairperson, the executive, and senior, respected board members approach the retreat.

Top-level commitment may be evidenced by actions such as:

♦ The board chairperson strongly endorses the retreat and becomes involved in the planning process;

♦ The chairperson appoints a Retreat Planning Committee, or specifically charges a standing committee with retreat-preparation responsibility;

- The retreat is planned far enough in advance so a date can be selected when most trustees are available;
- The executive becomes personally involved in retreat planning;
- The Retreat Planning Committee seeks board members' input through interviews or questionnaires;
- The board allocates a sufficient budget so the retreat's purposes are not compromised by inadequate facilities or support;
- Board members commit the time to prepare for and attend the retreat, recognizing that the retreat is just as important as participation at other board functions.

STEP 2: SET CLEAR AND REALISTIC GOALS AND OBJECTIVES

In general, a board retreat focuses on one or two main goals and a few objectives for achieving those goals. Any meeting that tries to cover too much is likely to disappoint. Some of the main goals addressed at retreats include: long-range or strategic planning, education on timely subjects, board self-assessment and development, and relationship-building. Specific retreat objectives flow from these broad goals.

Some retreat goals and objectives might include:

A. *Long-Range Planning*

   Typical objectives:
   1. Review and revise the organization's mission statement and vision for the future.
   2. Review recent strategic achievements, assess changes in the organization and its environment, and approve strategic aims for the future.

B. *Education on Timely Subjects*

   Typical objectives:
   1. Explore a significant topic, such as fund development, changing demographics, program expansion, or legislative issues and legal challenges, and examine the impact on the organization.

2. Take action related to the topic, such as board commitment to a capital campaign.

C. *Board Self-Assessment and Development*

Typical objectives:
1. Evaluate the board's roles, responsibilities, relationships, structure, work processes, recruitment mechanism, and overall effectiveness—and then identify opportunities for improvement.
2. Examine the relationships among the national board, regional boards, and local chapters.
3. Revise the organization's bylaws and committee structure.

D. *Relationship-Building*

Typical objectives:
1. Identify barriers to collaboration.
2. Improve communications, trust, and cohesiveness.
3. Strengthen the board-executive relationship.
4. Improve relations between the board and professional staff (hospital medical staff, university faculty).

Common Causes of Failure

Retreats fail to meet expectations for a variety of reasons, almost all of them preventable. Poor attendance is often cited, but it usually is a symptom of a flawed retreat planning process. Retreats fail when their goals and objectives are too broad or too vague, when they try to accomplish too much, or when the agenda presents just one speaker after another, with little or no time for board discussion. Retreats fail when selection of the goals and objectives, topics, and speakers is based on what one person thinks the board "ought to know," but the board itself is not consulted by means of a pre-retreat questionnaire or other planning tools. (See Appendix C for a Pre-Retreat Planning Questionnaire.) Finally, retreats can fail when the speaker, facilitator, or facility were not evaluated in advance, or because the time and place were ill-suited to board members' preferences and availability.

Many of these factors are at work in the following scenario:

For the annual Good Intentions Foundation Board Retreat, the chairperson and executive decided to focus on fund development. "We've got to get more trustees involved in fund-raising," they decided. An interesting speaker was invited, and the director of fund development presented a new fund-raising plan for board approval.

Many board members, however, didn't attend, and others said little during the retreat. The board approved the fund-raising plan, but the lack of discussion was disconcerting. In subsequent months, fund-raising faltered.

A fund-development consultant was brought in to conduct a confidential survey of board members. It turned out that many members were unclear or uncomfortable about the organization's mission. The board lacked a common vision of the future and, as a result, some members privately questioned the need for raising funds. The earlier board retreat had failed because it focused on the wrong goals. If the chairperson had appointed a representative planning committee, which had in turn commissioned a well-designed planning questionnaire, the underlying problems could have been discovered and then productively addressed at the retreat. Instead, valuable board time and fund-raising resources were squandered.

The Good Intentions scenario could have been avoided if, early in the planning process, the Retreat Planning Committee had solicited members' opinions and the executive's input as to desired goals and objectives, topics, speakers, time and place, etc. If professional leaders and experts are to be invited, then their input is needed as well. Merely assuming that the planning committee knows the needs and interests of participants is a prescription for failure.

STEP 3: RETREAT PREPARATION–LOGISTICS AND CONTENT

The Retreat Planning Committee is generally responsible for making substantive decisions; it should leave oversight of administrative tasks to the executive. The committee's purview includes:

♦ Developing and approving goals and objectives for the retreat;

- Developing an invitation list;
- Promoting attendance;
- Suggesting or approving timing and location;
- Selecting and approving speakers or a facilitator;
- Commenting on retreat instruments, such as questionnaires and agendas; and
- Coordinating retreat follow-up.

The executive is normally a member of, and staff to, the committee. Although planning of board retreats is a board responsibility, members must rely extensively on the executive for assistance on many fronts—from recommending retreat goals and objectives, to suggesting and contacting speakers, to coordinating facility arrangements. The executive should not be a passive participant in retreat planning, nor should he or she dominate it. A board retreat is board-directed and executive-executed. It should support the board's efforts, not impede them.

A. Invitation List

A retreat is sometimes limited to board members only, but very often other key individuals are invited, depending on the retreat goals and objectives. Some considerations are:

- *Chief executives.* Even if not a board member, the executive normally is invited. The executive is the board's leader-in-residence, and it is hard to imagine a retreat without him or her. The executive can be excused if executive assessment is on the agenda.

- *Other senior management and professional staff.* All parties essential to the retreat should be invited. Senior staff and professionals who interact regularly with the board may be invited if their presence will further the discussion and enhance the retreat objectives. For example, vice presidents frequently participate in strategic-planning retreats. Conversely, at board self-assessment retreats, the chief executive is often the only staff member who participates. The presence of managers other than the chief executive can inhibit frank board self-assessment. However, some boards invite the management team to join in a self-examination of the governance process, including board-management relationships. Such participation is usually a sign of mutual trust. The Retreat Planning Committee should decide which management should attend and the role senior staff will play: full participants, resource persons, group facilitators, or observers.

♦ *Spouses and guests.* Deciding whether to invite spouses sometimes causes controversy when planning a retreat. Some board members may object to the additional costs or the distraction from business. Boards of public agencies are especially sensitive to criticism of "junkets" at taxpayer expense. Nevertheless, there are good reasons to consider inviting spouses. If the retreat goals and objectives involve relationship-building, spouses can encourage socialization and break down barriers. Board members may be more willing to participate in longer retreats (i.e., two to three days) if spouses are invited. Finally, spouses endure a lot while their husbands or wives are engaged in board work; invitation to the retreat is a way of expressing appreciation. If spouses attend, consider scheduling activities for them during board sessions. Usually, spouses are invited to all receptions and meals, and sometimes to general sessions if the speaker and topic are of common interest.

Should the invitation extend only to spouses, or are guests also welcome? Again, this is an individual board decision. Today, with fewer "traditional" families, many boards leave it to individual trustees to decide if they will bring a guest. The category of retreat "guest" may include people with various ties to individual board members or the organization.

Who pays for the spouses and guests? That, too, is an individual board decision. Often, the organization pays for the guests' room and meals, and sometimes for travel.

Boards that are subject to "sunshine" or open meeting laws face a special challenge. The presence of the news media or the public may inhibit open and frank board discussion. Check with legal counsel to see what kinds of meetings could be exempt from the sunshine requirement. Often, the nature of a board retreat sounds dull to news reporters and they may opt not to cover it.

♦ *Honorary and emeritus trustees.* Usually, retreats are intended for the "working board." However, if honorary or emeritus trustees in fact remain involved in board activities, the Retreat Planning Committee can consider extending an invitation to them to attend. Conversely, if the titles honorary and emeritus are intended only to recognize prior service, it is not necessary to invite these former board members.

B. Timing and Location

Retreats should be scheduled as far in advance as possible, usually two to six months ahead of time. Seek the preferences of the board members and other participants for the best days of the week, desired locations, and times for starting and ending. Retreats can self-destruct because of failure to consult participants beforehand. For example:

> *The Good Intentions Foundation Retreat Planning Committee decided to start at 3 p.m. Friday afternoon, adjourn at 6 p.m. for dinner, and meet from 8 a.m. through noon on Saturday. At the appointed time, half the invited participants were missing. It turned out many were physicians in solo practice who often encountered unexpected patient visits on Friday afternoon. The Retreat Planning Committee had assumed erroneously that its time preference reflected everyone's schedule. A pre-retreat survey could have identified that an all-day Saturday or Saturday-Sunday retreat would have been preferable.*

The location of the retreat is important. Generally, it's a good idea to leave familiar territory, especially the boardroom. There, everyone sits in accustomed places and plays established roles. The open and relaxed discussion desired at a retreat is less likely. By getting at least an hour away, board members are less likely to be interrupted by beepers, quick trips to the office, phone calls, and other distractions. Overnight retreats help establish a retreat mindframe, receptive to new ideas and focused on the issues at hand.

The retreat setting should be conducive to discussion. Conference centers and hotels usually have good facilities. Look for comfortable meeting rooms, good audiovisual capabilities, small rooms for breakout sessions, and attractive grounds and recreational opportunities—especially golf, tennis, and hiking—for free time. (Yes, it's acceptable—even desirable—to schedule recreation time at a board retreat. Relationships are built at play as well as at work.)

C. Notification

Once the date and place are selected, send a written notice to all invitees as soon as possible. Some boards set their retreat dates a year in advance, while others find three to six months is adequate for members to commit to specific dates.

To stimulate interest, it's also useful to set the agenda and reading materials in advance. These tasks are usually done by the executive staff, in accordance with the overall direction of the Retreat Planning Committee.

Invitees should be asked to reply promptly. Executive staff should follow-up, if necessary, with non-respondents. If key players do not respond or plan not to attend, an appropriate, influential leader (board chairperson, Retreat Planning Chair, or executive) can contact these individuals and explain why their participation is important.

How big a turnout is enough to proceed? Generally, less than 50 percent means postponement. Attendance of 80 to 100 percent is common at successful retreats.

D. Speakers and Facilitators

Good speakers stimulate thinking by bringing their expertise, insight, and fresh information to the board. Speakers may come from inside and outside the organization. Do not allow speakers to dominate. Build into the agenda opportunities for question-and-answer sessions and board problem-solving.

Provocative and informative presentations contribute to achieving retreat goals and objectives. To this end, some boards employ a facilitator, an individual experienced in planning and conducting board retreats. Some speakers are skilled facilitators and serve double duty. Facilitators can:

- Inject objectivity and experience into retreat planning, data-gathering, and discussion at the meeting;
- Allow the chairperson to participate freely, without the responsibility to conduct the meeting;
- Keep the discussion moving and stimulate participation, without allowing any one person to dominate;
- Use various group-process and team-building techniques;
- Play devil's advocate, encouraging the board to discuss uncomfortable but important issues;

- Play peacemaker, and keep conflict from turning destructive;
- Drive the retreat toward closure;
- Prepare a post-retreat summary; and
- Assist the board after the retreat to implement recommendations or plan future retreats.

Boards conducting their first retreat, and boards that need to build communications, relationships, and trust, are usually well-served by expert facilitators. Strategic-planning and board self-assessment retreats may also benefit from an outsider's guidance and perspective. Always check professional references before choosing a facilitator. If a facilitator is retained, involve him or her as early as possible in the retreat-planning process. Provide background information on the organization (e.g., bylaws, mission, other key documents). Facilitators can be helpful in designing the pre-retreat questionnaire and creating the agenda.

Someone must run the retreat. Therefore, if an outside facilitator is not used, someone inside the organization must lead the discussion. Often, this is the board chairperson or executive. A disadvantage here is that having the usual authority figures run the meeting could inhibit discussion. It's business as usual. Even more important, the facilitator cannot be both participant and facilitator: it's one role or the other. Thus, if the chairperson or executive wants to be actively involved in shaping the new mission or contributing to board self-assessment, someone else should serve as facilitator.

STEP 4: GATHERING DATA

If there is a secret to successful retreats, it is advance data-gathering. The following kinds of data are generally pertinent:

- Environmental data on trends and new developments that could or do affect the organization's future;
- Organizational data on key performance indicators, such as finances, service volumes, program growth, human resources; and
- Perception data, generally based on pre-retreat surveys of the board, executive management, professional staff, or the

community-at-large. (Such information is distinct from the retreat planning questionnaire discussed earlier.)

Good data replace opinion and anecdotes with objective assessment. Some data-gathering is done to help the facilitator or Retreat Planning Committee custom-design the retreat goals, objectives, and agenda. Some data (such as financial trends and other environmental or organizational data) are intended for *advance* dissemination, so trustees can brief themselves prior to the retreat. Other types of data (such as self-evaluation questionnaire results) are best presented *at* the retreat, where they can be explained and discussed in-depth.

The types of data gathered depend on the focus of the retreat. For example, strategic-planning and board-development retreats call for different types of data, as described below.

Strategic Planning

Strategy retreats generally require information that gives the board the big picture of key trends and factors affecting future achievement of the organization's mission. To help a board examine its mission, vision, and strategy, information might include:

♦ Financial trends;

♦ Demographic changes;

♦ New technology or research findings;

♦ Competition; and

♦ Legislative and regulatory trends.

Board Development and Leadership Relationships

Retreats concerning board self-evaluation, board development, or leadership relationships also benefit from pre-retreat questionnaires or interviews. Confidential data-gathering can identify issues that board members are reluctant to discuss openly, such as problems in board-executive relationships or the role of the board chairperson. Instead of a member being forced to raise these sensitive topics individually, a skilled facilitator can use questionnaire results to introduce them in a depersonalized, nonthreatening manner.

Personal interviews are sometimes used instead of, or in addition to, written questionnaires. Interviews are appropriate when there is concern that respondents will be reluctant to complete a questionnaire frankly, or when a questionnaire is unlikely to identify festering concerns or root causes of conflict. Both interviews and questionnaires are best administered by an objective outsider, such as the retreat facilitator. Trustees are more likely to offer honest responses if they know their individual answers will be confidential. Questionnaires should be returned *directly* to the facilitator, and not be processed by the Retreat Planning Committee or executive office. The facilitator is responsible for preparing aggregate results to share with the board. If a facilitator is not used, and the questionnaires are returned to the Planning Committee or executive, preserve anonymity by giving all trustees identical, postage-paid return envelopes and by having members omit writing their names on their questionnaires.

STEP 5: THE RETREAT ITSELF

A retreat agenda usually has several main components: ice-breaking and socializing, buy-in, content, discussion, closure, and follow-up action.

- *Ice-breaking and socializing.* Retreats offer an opportunity to build relationships, educate and involve new trustees, and enhance the board's ability to work as a team. People work best in groups when they are relaxed and comfortable with each other. The ice-breaker could be a social event that precedes the formal session, or a group exercise that starts the meeting. When boards charter a bus or other transportation to a retreat, the trip itself acts as ice breaker, and the board arrives ready to go.

- *Buy-in.* The "buy-in" is a short, subtle, but important part of the meeting. It occurs when the chair or facilitator describes the retreat planning process goals, objectives, and agenda, and then asks the group: *"Does everyone agree with these objectives?"* and *"Should anything else be on the agenda?"*

  If the retreat planning has been done well and is based on data from questionnaires and other sources, the board should quickly recognize and accept—buy-into—the appropriateness of the goals, objectives, and agenda.

  But what if members raise objections or start adding new agenda items? Hasn't control of the retreat been lost at the outset? Not in the hands of a good facilitator. The facilitator may incorporate new agenda items if they are pertinent and achievable, or list them on a flip chart labelled "Items for the Future." Similarly, a skilled facilitator knows how to deal diplomatically with meeting participants who crusade, monopolize, or otherwise disrupt the flow of the meeting.

Beginning the meeting with a skillful buy-in discussion (on goals, objectives, and agenda) signals participants that the purpose of the meeting is open and not hidden. Members know the democratic process is at work, everyone's views will be heard, and that the facilitator is there to channel the meeting to a productive conclusion.

- *Content.* The content could include outside speakers, inside speakers, questionnaire results, and so forth. In general, it's a good idea to keep formal speeches to a minimum. Allow as much opportunity as possible for discussion. Overstructuring the format will discourage the board members' participation.

- *Discussion.* Case exercises and small discussion groups are good tools for increasing involvement. The ideal size of a discussion group is about six to nine, big enough for diversity but small enough so everyone has a chance to participate. If a retreat is larger than about 15 members, consider dividing into smaller groups when the agenda comes to brainstorming or developing action ideas. Give the groups a specific task (e.g., *"Which board committees can we eliminate?"*) and a time limit. Then, reconvene the entire board, have each group report, and summarize the recommendations on a flip chart. After each small group reports, open the topic for general discussion and aim at, if possible, consensus.

- *Closure.* The closure of a meeting is important. If the retreat is designed to generate specific actions or decisions, the facilitator may help the group to summarize an action plan to expedite follow-up. (A good action plan clearly states what will be done, who has responsibility for follow-up, and when results are expected. See Appendix D.) The board chairperson usually has the last word, thanking the board for its participation and reaffirming his or her initial commitment to the retreat process. End the retreat on a high note. Even if the retreat is not intended to produce definite actions, the facilitator, chairperson, or executive should summarize the discussions briefly.

STEP 6: POST-RETREAT ACTION

A post-retreat evaluation questionnaire may be sent to participants for assessing results and planning the next retreat. The results of a retreat are both tangible and intangible. The tangible results, which might be a new mission statement or recommendations to eliminate superfluous committees, should be written in the action plan for follow-up after the retreat.

As a rule, the board takes no votes and makes no official decisions at a retreat. Voting detracts from the open, participative, relaxed atmosphere. Formal votes should be left for subsequent business meetings. The post-retreat interval can also be used for staff or committees to clean up loose ends. Many a mission statement that looked brilliant on a flip chart at the end of a long, hard retreat sounds a little less clear the next day. Before the board votes, the executive or chairperson can make modest edits in the words but not the meaning.

A retreat's intangible results are equally important and fulfilling. Board members often say a retreat deepened their understanding of the organization and introduced new perspectives. Typical post-retreat comments are: "I wasn't aware of the sort of problems management faces" or "I thought Jack was just being difficult, but now I understand what he's saying." A retreat rejuvenates and restores; it builds spirit and teamwork.

CONCLUSION

What is the key to a successful retreat? Is it a hard-working planning committee, dynamic speakers, an agreeable locale, a skilled facilitator, or an executive who carries out preparation down to the last detail? All these factors are important, but if a key factor must be chosen, it would be a planning process that involves board members.

Board members feel that retreat time is well spent when they make clear progress on significant issues and working relationships. Boards know what the important issues are—but there is often no time to discuss them during routine board activities. An effective retreat-planning process surfaces the critical issues and builds the agenda around them. When members are vested in retreat planning, the retreat will be a success. In turn, a successful retreat is an investment in the ongoing process of building an excellent board that contributes to organizational success.

APPENDIX A

Retreat Planning Process

1
Secure Commitment from the Board Leadership, All Members and the Executive

6
Follow-Up Retreat Recommendations

2
Set Clear and Realistic Objectives

5
Conduct the Retreat and Develop an Action Plan

3
Prepare Content and Logistic Details

4
Gather Pertinent Data
(e.g., self-assessment questionnaire)

APPENDIX B

Board Retreat Checklist

Item:	Assigned To:	Date Due:
COMMITMENT		
☐ Board Chairperson's Endorsement		
☐ Executive Personally Involved		
☐ Planning Committee Assigned		
☐ Pre-Retreat Questionnaire Mailed		
OBJECTIVE-SETTING		
☐ Specific Objectives Adopted		
☐ Objectives Based on Questionnaire or Other Diagnostic Tool		
☐ Objectives are Clear and Realistic		
☐ Objectives are Communicated to Full Board		
PLANNING AND PREPARATION		
☐ Invitation List Developed		
☐ Present Board Members and Executive		
☐ Honorary/Emeritus Trustees?		
☐ Spouses and Guests?		
☐ Senior Management?		
☐ Professional Staff		
☐ Others?		
☐ Choose Retreat Site, Considering:		
☐ Distance		
☐ Meeting Facilities		
☐ Recreational Opportunities		
☐ Cost		
☐ Choose Time and Length of Retreat		
☐ Choose Speakers (if desired)		

Item:	Assigned To:	Date Due:

☐ Choose Facilitator (if desired) _____ _____

☐ Have Facilitator Meet with Planning Committee _____ _____

☐ Verify Logistical Details:
☐ Travel _____ _____
☐ Sleeping Room (early/late checkout) _____ _____
☐ Program for Spouses and Guests _____ _____
☐ Receptions and Meals _____ _____
☐ Audiovisual Needs (e.g., projectors, flipcharts) _____ _____
☐ Participant Materials Packets: Advance _____ _____
☐ Participant Materials Packets: At Meeting _____ _____

DATA-GATHERING

☐ Obtain Input from Board Members _____ _____
☐ Pre-Retreat Questionnaire _____ _____
☐ Interviews _____ _____
☐ Planning Committee _____ _____
☐ Prepare Background Information _____ _____

MEETING DYNAMICS

☐ Prepare Agenda that Matches Retreat Objectives _____ _____
☐ Ensure the Agenda Balances Presentations with Board Activity _____ _____
☐ Mix Work Time, Socializing, Recreation, and Free Time _____ _____

Planning Successful Board Retreats

Item:	Assigned To:	Date Due:
FOLLOW-UP ACTIONS		
❏ Prepare Action Plan	_____	_____
❏ Disseminate Plan to All Participants	_____	_____
❏ Follow-Up on Plan	_____	_____
❏ Disseminate and Tally Retreat Evaluation Survey	_____	_____
❏ Schedule the Next Retreat	_____	_____

APPENDIX C

Pre-Retreat Planning Questionnaire

Dear (*Retreat Participant*):

To assist in the planning of this year's retreat, please take a moment to complete this brief questionnaire. Return by (*insert date*) to the Retreat Planning Committee or to the Retreat Facilitator (*indicate whichever is appropriate*).

1. Are you a member of: (circle all that apply)
   Board   Administration   Professional Staff

2. Listed below are *suggested* objectives for this year's retreat. Please rank your order of preference (1, 2, 3, etc., with 1 being the highest ranking).

   _____ To learn more about the challenges facing our organization in today's environment.

   _____ To discuss strategic directions our organization should take in the future.

   _____ To evaluate the board's performance and identify opportunities for improvement.

   _____ To discuss the relationship between the board and executive staff, and how the relationship could be improved to mutual benefit.

   _____ Other objectives: _____

---

3. Listed below are potential topics for this year's retreat. Please rank them in your order of preference (1, 2, 3, etc.):

   _____ Board/Management Roles, Relationships, and Communications

   _____ Fund Raising

   _____ Progress in Achieving Strategic Objectives and Goals

   _____ Institutional Programs

   _____ Community Relations

____ Update on Financial Trends and Other Environmental Forces

____ Tax-Exempt Status

____ Other: _____

4. Of the topics above, which *two* should receive the greatest emphasis at the retreat:

    #1 _____

    #2 _____

5. My suggestions for speakers include:

6. My preference for a location would be (1, 2, 3, etc.):

    ____ Grand Hotel

    ____ Country Club

    ____ College

    ____ Conference Center

    ____ Boardroom

    ____ Other: _____

7. My preference for time would be (1, 2, 3, etc.):

    ____ Friday Night/Saturday

    ____ Saturday/Sunday

    ____ Weekday

    ____ (Best Day: _____)

8. Other comments: _____

Appendix D

Sample Action Plan

Action:	Who Expedites:	By When:
1. STRATEGIC PLANNING *Mission Statement:* The mission was generally reaffirmed as being an accurate, current statement of our reason for being. A number of wording changes were suggested.	Planning Committee and management to revise and submit to board.	Next board meeting.
Strategic Plan: Broaden strategic plan to reflect longer-term (3–5 years) vision and its major strategic goals. Continue evolution of strategic-planning process as a tool for board-management communication, priority-setting, and decision-making.	Planning Committee.	Draft ready for year-end review.

Action:	Who Expedites:	By When:
2. BOARD DEVELOPMENT		
Board Meetings: Focus board time more on issues, not maintenance (e.g., finance reports). Reduce "canned" presentation time. Use board calendar to schedule policy issues for discussion.	Board Chairperson/ Chief Executive.	Calendar in place by January.
Conflict Management: Make board aware of potential opposition and conflicts when it reviews major proposals, and inform board if conflicts have or can be resolved.	Board Chairperson/ Chief Executive.	On-going.

APPENDIX E

Sample Board Retreat Agendas

1. DAY AND A HALF BOARD RETREAT

Location:	Conference Center about 2 hours from home
Objectives:	To begin the process of developing a long-range, strategic plan
	To continue the process of building communication, trust, and a common sense of mission and vision among board, senior management, and professional staff
Invitees:	Board members, senior executive staff, senior professional staff

Day One

12-2 p.m.	Hotel check-in/Lunch on your own
2:00	Welcome
	Board chairperson
	Self-introductions by participants
2:30	Opening Remarks: Challenges and opportunities in the coming decade
	Guest speaker
	Questions and discussion
3:30	Break
3:45	Introduction of facilitator
	Review of the organization's mission
	Participants divide into small groups of 6-8 persons each. The groups select a spokesperson and a recorder. They then review the current mission statement and make recommendations for change, if any.

	Small groups report/discussion and consensus on the mission
	Each small group reports its conclusions. The facilitator helps the group reach consensus, and in the process, promotes discussion about the true meaning of the organization's mission.
6:00	Session adjourns
7:00	Reception and dinner for participants and guests

Day Two

7:30 a.m.	Breakfast
8:30	Developing a vision
	The facilitator explains the difference between a mission (why we exist) and a vision (a description of the organization that will achieve the mission in the future).
10:00	Break
	Vision exercise
	The facilitator leads a vision exercise that helps participants identify areas of agreement and disagreement over their vision for the future. The group then sets priorities as to which areas are most important to discuss.
12:00 p.m.	Lunch
1:00	Small group discussions on vision
	Small groups discuss the priority areas and develop recommendations for a vision statement.
	Development of a vision statement
	Small groups report. The facilitator seeks to develop consensus around a vision statement that represents a common view of board, senior management, and professional staff.

2:30 Break

2:45 Action planning/linkage to the strategic planning process

The facilitator asks participants to recommend specific actions that will be considered by planning staff and the Retreat Committee as they develop a strategic plan over the next several months. The board will hold another retreat to review, discuss, and approve the strategic plan.

4:00 Retreat adjourns

2. ONE DAY BOARD RETREAT

Location: Downtown Conference Center

Objectives: To evaluate and improve the board's structure and performance

To continue the process of building an effective relationship between the board and the chief executive

Invitees: Board members and CEO

7:30 a.m. Breakfast

8:30 Welcome

Board chairperson

Self-introductions by participants

Introduction of facilitator

Opening Remarks: What makes an effective board retreat facilitator

Questions and discussion

10:00 Break

Presentation and discussion of self-evaluation questionnaires (completed and returned by board members to facilitator prior to retreat)

Identification of priority issues for discussion/areas needing improvement

12:00 p.m.   Lunch

1:00   Discussion of priority issues for discussion/areas needing improvement

The facilitator leads this discussion. If the board has 15 or more members, it may be advisable to divide into smaller groups for an initial discussion, and then reconvene for a general discussion.

3:00   Break

3:15   Action planning
The board agrees on specific actions for improvement (see Action Plan, Appendix D).

4:30   Retreat adjourns

Notes: 1. The times on retreat agendas must be viewed flexibly. A retreat is a dynamic process. Some topics may require more discussion than anticipated, while other issues may achieve consensus easily. It is the facilitator's responsibility to permit sufficient discussion and still move the group toward a conclusion.

2. The paragraphs in italic type describe the conduct of the retreat in detail and are meant to guide the retreat facilitator. Usually, these are not included in the agenda disseminated to participants.

SUGGESTED RESOURCES

Bader, Barry S. *Five Keys to Building an Excellent Board.* Rockville, MD: Bader & Associates, Inc., 1991.

This book describes five principles of ongoing board development, and illustrates them with case examples. The book emphasizes the selection, display, and use of board information, and offers numerous sample formats. Although oriented toward boards of healthcare organizations, the publication has generic applicability.

Ingram, Richard T. *Trustee Orientation and Development Programs.* Washington, D.C.: Association of Governing Boards of Universities and Colleges, 2nd edition, 1989, 11 pages.

This booklet offers a quick and practical guide to setting up orientation programs, workshops, and retreats for trustees at colleges and universities.

Savage, R. J. "Trustees at the Crossroads: Strengthening Their Future Position." *Health Progress*, May 1988, pp. 33-36.

This article discusses the use of retreats in the context of a board focusing on future strategies. Oriented toward boards of Catholic organizations.

Slesinger, Larry H. *Self-Assessment for Nonprofit Governing Boards.* Washington, D.C.: National Center for Nonprofit Boards, 1991.

This facilitator handbook with individual board member questionnaires will help boards analyze their own strengths and weaknesses and identify areas of board action where better performance would help the board become a more effective governing body. The package is suitable for a broad range of nonprofit boards. The critical process of conducting a successful board self-assessment is described, including the important role of an organizing task force of board members and the use of an outside facilitator to interpret the questionnaire's data and to guide a constructive meeting to discuss the results with the full board.

Swanson, Andrew. "Planning a Board Retreat." *Nonprofit World*, Jan./Feb. 1989, Vol. 7, No. 1, p. 1920.

This article discusses the advantages of board retreats and how to make them successful. The author emphasizes the value of getting away from distractions in order to think about the future. He calls advance retreat planning a "necessity."

Umbdenstock, Richard J., Winifred M. Hageman, and Barry S. Bader. *Improving and Evaluating Board Performance.* Rockville, MD: Bader & Associates, Inc., 1986, 84 pages.

Designed as pre-retreat reading for a hospital board engaging in self-assessment, this book puts trustees at ease about the self-evaluation process and offers ideas for improving the board, including board profiles, recruitment plans, and a Governance Committee.

ABOUT THE AUTHOR

Barry S. Bader, president of Bader & Associates, Inc., of Rockville, Maryland, is a consultant, speaker, and author specializing in governance, leadership development, and quality improvement with an emphasis in the healthcare field. He is publisher of *THE QUALITY LETTER for Healthcare Leaders*, the only healthcare-quality publication written for trustees, senior executives, and physician leaders. Mr. Bader is a member of the board of trustees of Suburban Hospital, Bethesda, Maryland, and chairman of its medical affairs committee. He has also written several books and articles about boards and healthcare issues.